11+ English

For GL Assessment

This CGP book is brilliant for children aged 9-10 who are working towards the GL 11+. It's set at a slightly easier level than the real test — perfect for building confidence.

The first few sections are packed with topic-based questions that'll help them get to grips with each crucial skill. Once they've mastered those, they can move on to the mixed-topic Assessment Tests for more realistic 11+ practice.

There's also a detailed pull-out Answer Book to make marking as simple as possible!

How to access your free Online Edition

This book includes a free Online Edition to read on your PC, Mac or tablet. You'll just need to go to **cgpbooks.co.uk/extras** and enter this code:

4162 5976 1453 2068

By the way, this code only works for one person. If somebody else has used this book before you, they might have already claimed the Online Edition.

Practice Book – Ages 9-10

with Assessment Tests

How to use this Practice Book

This book is divided into two parts — themed question practice and assessment tests.
There are answers and detailed explanations in the pull-out answer book.

Themed question practice

- Each page contains practice questions divided by topic. Use these pages to work out your child's strengths and the areas they find tricky. The questions get harder down each page.
- Your child can use the smiley face tick boxes to evaluate how confident they feel with each topic.

Assessment tests

- The second half of the book contains six assessment tests, each with two comprehension texts and a matching set of questions, as well as a set of questions on grammar, spelling and punctuation. They take a similar form to the real test.
- You can print off multiple choice answer sheets from cgpbooks.co.uk/11plus/answer-sheets, so your child can practise taking the tests as if they're sitting the real thing.
- Use the printable answer sheets if you want your child to do each test more than once.
- If you want to give your child timed practice, give them a time limit of 40 minutes for each test, and ask them to work as quickly and carefully as they can.
- The tests get harder from 1-6, so don't be surprised if your child finds the later ones more tricky.
- Your child should aim for a mark of around 85% (34 questions correct) in each test. If they score less than this, use their results to work out the areas they need more practice on.
- If they haven't managed to finish the test in time, they need to work on increasing their speed, whereas if they have made a lot of mistakes, they need to work more carefully.
- Keep track of your child's scores using the progress chart on the inside back cover of the book.

Published by CGP

Editors:
Claire Boulter, Heather Gregson, Anthony Muller, Holly Poynton, Jo Sharrock

Contributors:
Alison Griffin, Steve Martin, Julie Moxon, Tina Ramsden, Lucy Towle

With thanks to Jennifer Underwood and Janet Berkeley for the proofreading.

With thanks to Jane Ellingham for the copyright research.

ISBN: 978 1 78908 154 1

Printed by Elanders Ltd, Newcastle upon Tyne
Clipart from Corel®

Based on the classic CGP style created by Richard Parsons.

Contents

Section One — Grammar

Parts of Speech .... 2 ✓
Verbs .... 4 ☐
Mixed Grammar Questions .... 6 ☐

Tick off the check box for each topic as you go along.

Section Two — Punctuation

Starting and Ending Sentences .... 8 ☐
Commas and Brackets .... 9 ☐
Dashes and Apostrophes .... 10 ☐
Inverted Commas and Colons .... 11 ☐
Mixed Punctuation Questions .... 12 ☐

Section Three — Spelling

Plurals .... 14 ☐
Homophones .... 15 ☐
Prefixes and Suffixes .... 16 ☐
Awkward Spellings .... 17 ☐
Mixed Spelling Questions .... 18 ☐

Section Four — Writers' Techniques

Alliteration and Onomatopoeia .... 20 ☐
Imagery .... 21 ☐
Abbreviations .... 22 ☐
Synonyms and Antonyms .... 23 ☐
Spotting and Understanding Devices .... 24 ☐

Section Five — Writing

Writing Fiction .... 26 ☐
Writing Non-Fiction .... 28 ☐

Assessment Tests

Test 1 .... 30 ☐
Test 2 .... 38 ☐
Test 3 .... 46 ☐
Test 4 .... 54 ☐
Test 5 .... 62 ☐
Test 6 .... 70 ☐

Glossary 78

Parts of Speech

Nouns

Write down whether the word in bold is a proper noun, a collective noun, a common noun or an abstract noun. For example:

The **flock** of sheep wandered into the road. collective noun

1. The infamous family portrait was in an antique **frame**. ____________
2. I was born in **Paris**, the capital city of France. ____________
3. **Cassie** shows kindness to everyone, even her brother. ____________
4. A **school** of dolphins swam past our boat. ____________
5. **Knowledge** is the key to success in life. ____________
6. The school bullies looked like a **pack** of wolves. ____________
7. Her tent flapped in the **wind** and the rain poured in. ____________
8. We're going away to get some rest and **relaxation**. ____________

/ 8

Pronouns

Choose the correct pronoun to replace the word or words in bold and write it on the line. For example:

The red picnic blanket was **Jennifer and Kirat's**. theirs

Hint: Think about whether the pronoun shows possession — if it does, you'll need to use words like 'ours' or 'theirs'.

9. **Louise** fed the swans and their cygnets yesterday. ____________
10. **Cathleen and I** will catch the bus into town. ____________
11. Zara ran to close **the window** as the rain began to fall. ____________
12. **Vinay** held his breath as he swam under the water. ____________
13. This wooden ruler is **Monika's**. ____________
14. The broken terracotta pot belongs to **Dad**. ____________
15. The Shetland pony is **mine and Glenda's**. ____________
16. The self-portraits on the wall are **Iona and Tom's**. ____________

/ 8

Parts of Speech

Adjectives & Adverbs

Write down whether the word in bold is an adverb or an adjective. For example:

The gardener grew a **beautiful** rose. adjective

Hint: Remember, adjectives describe nouns, and adverbs describe verbs and adjectives.

1. He shouted **excitedly** when his favourite team scored. ____________
2. Pritam bought **pink** balloons for his younger sister. ____________
3. Ivan will **probably** win the competition. ____________
4. The ninja hamster was a **daring** performer. ____________
5. This summer's forest fire was **very** dangerous. ____________
6. He had to run **fast** to escape the angry bull. ____________
7. Mr Petinski's moustache was **bristly**. ____________
8. '**Thirsty**' didn't even begin to describe how Nigel felt. ____________

/ 8

Prepositions

Complete these sentences by adding the correct preposition. Choose from: **above**, **below**, **through** and **into**. For example:

Marianne fell into the lake.

9. The multicoloured mobile was hung ________ the cot so that the baby could see it.
10. The passengers leapt ________ the basket of the hot air balloon before it took off.
11. A cricket ball crashed ________ the window and into the kitchen.
12. We sat on the top of the hill and looked at the village ________ us.
13. To reach the railway station, turn left and go ________ the stone archway.
14. We were high ________ the city and the pedestrians looked like ants to us.
15. Wendy bought a raffle ticket which went ________ the grand prize draw.
16. The celebrity cut ________ the ribbon to open the new hospital.

/ 8

Verbs

Verbs

Underline the verb in each sentence. For example:

James <u>hired</u> a tuxedo for the party.

1. The last show of the day begins in ten minutes' time.
2. Hattie often helps me with my homework, especially maths.
3. Bhat's elaborate excuses impressed the class, but not the teacher.
4. They heard a strange whispering noise behind them, then silence.
5. I spilt my popcorn all over a stranger in the cinema on Saturday.
6. In that respect, last winter's pantomime was a success.
7. I have many wild flowers in my garden, including dandelions.
8. The phone's shrill ring took me completely by surprise.

Hint: Watch out for words that are spelt the same as verbs, but are nouns or adjectives.

/ 8

Verbs

Change the verb in bold so that it is in the correct tense. For example:

Kim **gone** to karate class last Sunday. <u>went</u>

9. Matt still gets annoyed when people **didn't** tidy up. ______
10. Beth felt quite travel sick when she **flies** to Australia. ______
11. I **go** to the theme park with my cousins yesterday. ______
12. He was annoyed when the dog **knocks** over his drink. ______
13. My dad can **spoke** six languages, including Mandarin. ______
14. My goldfish was delighted when she **passes** her driving test. ______
15. I **leave** my P.E. kit in the changing rooms last week. ______
16. "Take that back!" Amara **say**, as she slammed the door. ______

/ 8

Verbs

Verbs

Underline the correct verb from the brackets to complete each sentence. For example:

Andy (is were be) going to the park today.

1. Cerys **(went goes gone)** to the doctor's last night.
2. Blacksmiths have **(making make made)** horseshoes for centuries.
3. Divyesh is **(have going having)** a bouncy-castle party on Sunday afternoon.
4. I **(was is had)** just finishing my homework when the doorbell rang.
5. "It has **(broken broke break)**!" cried Mahmud mournfully.
6. The sailor **(talk talked talks)** about her time at sea until the sun rose.

/ 6

7. Grace **(will has is)** fall over and land in the mud.
8. Corned beef makes me **(feel feeling felt)** ill.
9. The choir had **(sang sings sung)** the piece many times before.
10. He **(drives driven drove)** to school in a go-kart yesterday.
11. My nephew **(would can will)** have been there if I had asked him.
12. Once Ben **(begins begun began)** writing the story, he couldn't stop.

/ 6

13. I **(sees saw seen)** where the group of runners went.
14. It **(is were was)** forbidden to enter the courtyard when the gate was shut.
15. She **(hears hear heard)** the steam train before she could see it.
16. Salami **(is are were)** a type of cured meat eaten with bread.
17. Lottie watched the spider **(spin spun spins)** its web.
18. I **(bought brought buys)** these apples at the market.

/ 6

Mixed Grammar Questions

Underline the word in each sentence which matches the part of speech in brackets. For example:

Rachel rushed over to help. **(noun)**

1. Aisha enjoyed cycling slowly around the duck pond. **(adverb)**
2. We decided to eat our picnic under the large beech tree. **(preposition)**
3. The long-haired ginger dragon was often prowling around. **(noun)**
4. We travelled to Hawaii with our pet mouse and a supply of sausages. **(verb)**
5. Are you going to swim across the English Channel? **(preposition)**
6. We're going to put up our old tent in the garden and have a sleepover. **(adjective)**
7. When I was five, I accidentally fell out of a bedroom window. **(adverb)**
8. Melinda, who has blonde hair, is my new sister-in-law. **(relative pronoun)**

/ 8

Write down whether the word in bold is a noun, verb, preposition, adjective or adverb. For example:

He **works** at the weekends. verb

9. The caring **nurse** tended to her infirm patient. ____________
10. I was lucky to **dance** the tango and the rumba with Alejandro. ____________
11. **Listen** carefully to all the instructions before you begin. ____________
12. She is an **impressive** chess player, but she won't beat Peter. ____________
13. **Suddenly**, the boat capsized and we were thrown into the sea. ____________
14. I don't know the answer — can I have a **clue**? ____________
15. The tiny black kitten scrambled **into** the box. ____________
16. He pulled the rope **harder** to tighten the knot. ____________

/ 8

Mixed Grammar Questions

Underline the most appropriate word from the brackets to complete each sentence. For example:

Brian went out **(because despite to during)** it had stopped raining.

1. I am going to watch TV **(during so yet until)** Nassrin arrives.
2. When I forgot my pen, Zoe said I could **(borrowed borrow borrows lend)** one of hers.
3. He **(slowly fast quick slower)** raised his hand to answer the question.
4. Luke used to **(love loved loves enjoyed)** eating pancakes for breakfast.
5. I was grateful for his **(thought thoughtful thinking thoughts)** present.
6. I always wondered **(that what which when)** lay beyond the mansion's gates.

/ 6

7. I **(finding found find finds)** the day at the museum interesting.
8. When we made paper lanterns, the glue **(sticks sticky stuck sticked)** to my fingers.
9. We had to pass **(through around into on)** a security scanner to reach the departure lounge.
10. Of all my friends, I know you the **(well best good better)**.
11. Tamara won the trophy; it was **(their hers her its)** third victory this year.
12. I cracked the egg **(into through around to)** the cake batter.

/ 6

13. My teacher looked **(seriously serious angrily seriousness)** when he told me to stop talking.
14. When my family go on holiday, we take **(our their are ours)** own towels.
15. **(During Although Despite However)** I had a fever, I came first in the egg and spoon race.
16. Kerry threw the ball, then the whistle blew: the trophy was **(their theirs they're these)**.
17. Manjit **(bought brought bring buys)** crisps and sandwiches to the garden party.
18. The play **(that what who whose)** we watched today was longer than last week's.

/ 6

Starting and Ending Sentences

Read the passage below. Draw a circle where you would add a capital letter and add a full stop where you would end each sentence.
For example:

Penguins only live in the southern hemisphere.

1. the spectacular northern lights take place near the North Pole bright coloured lights appear when conditions are right and illuminate the night sky these patterns are most commonly green but can be pink or blue it is a phenomenon that is rarely observed as far south as the United Kingdom

/ 4

2. for around 200 years, people in a Gloucestershire village have taken part in an annual cheese-rolling event when the race starts, a round block of Double Gloucester is rolled down a slope while competitors race after it the first person to the bottom wins the cheese such an unusual event brings many visitors to the area

/ 4

Write out these sentences so that they start and finish correctly.
For example:

are we nearly there yet   Are we nearly there yet?

Hint: These sentences could end with a question mark, an exclamation mark or a full stop.

3. she couldn't understand the question

____

4. what a surprise this is

____

5. who could resist this opportunity

____

6. when he left the room, I could relax

____

/ 4

Commas and Brackets

Brackets

Each of these sentences is missing a pair of brackets. Add brackets around the correct information in each sentence. For example:

Miss Jones (our teacher) read a story.

1. My best friend Jonny Parker gave a speech in assembly .
2. I love playing tennis my favourite sport during the summer .
3. Peter Chloe's uncle enjoys bird-watching at the weekend .
4. The entrance fee is £2 for children free for children under 4 .
5. My stepsister works for the N.T.P.A. National Tortoise Protection Association .
6. The dogs Max and Buster couldn't wait to go for a walk .
7. Yashbal lives in the centre of town Hartley Road .
8. Most nouns naming words can be made plural .

Hint: The sentence should still make sense if the words in the brackets are removed.

/ 8

Commas

Circle the incorrect comma in each sentence. For example:

Wendy had sweets, cake, and jelly at her party.

9. When I was seventeen, we went ice-skating, all the time.
10. Hepzibah, the best baker in the village, always made, tasty sponge cakes.
11. Before leaving, you, should make sure that it is safe.
12. Eilean had a mansion with a pool, a verandah, a cinema and, a jacuzzi.
13. The child, who was four at the time, played the piano, really well.
14. Miss Cheetham, our form tutor, is getting married, on Saturday.
15. Meena, wearing a navy, blue coat, was waiting outside the school.
16. Paris has many, beautiful sights, including the river, galleries and parks.

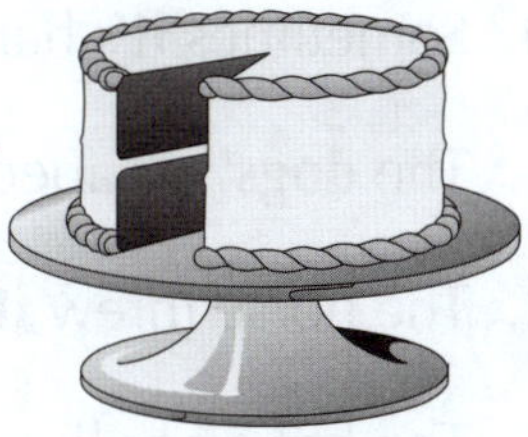

/ 8

Dashes and Apostrophes

Dashes

Each of these sentences is missing a pair of dashes. Add dashes around the correct information in each sentence. For example:

Crackers — the pet shop's oldest parrot — finally found a home.

1. The Eiffel Tower a monument in Paris was once the tallest structure in Europe.
2. I picked a glass vase one with a painting of fish on it for the living room.
3. After crossing the bridge the only way to get over the river we headed north.
4. The farmer who was very reckless chased the herd of llamas.
5. The dolphin the largest adult in the pod surfed the incoming waves.
6. Patch and Fungus my two beagles barked at the children.

/ 6

Apostrophes

Each word in bold has an apostrophe. If the apostrophe is used correctly, write N on the line. If the apostrophe is used incorrectly, write the word out correctly on the line. For example:

My **grannys'** tent is extremely waterproof. granny's

Hint: You may need to rewrite the word with the apostrophe in a different place, or remove it altogether.

7. I was ill so I **didn't** go to school today. ____________
8. **Youl'l** need to run to catch the bus. ____________
9. You **must'nt** go to the fun-fair by yourself. ____________
10. Sometimes **it's** hard not to be a bad loser. ____________
11. The **dogs'** escaped from the garden. ____________
12. The horse threw **its** rider off during the race. ____________
13. The hot air balloon landed in **Sui's** garden. ____________
14. The **childrens'** shoes were covered in mud. ____________
15. Broadway is famous for **it's** theatres. ____________
16. We walked along the **waters'** edge. ____________

/ 10

Inverted Commas and Colons

Inverted Commas

Rewrite this reported speech as direct speech. For example:

Mum commented that she likes the green one.
"I like the green one," commented Mum.

1. Karolina politely asked where the toilets are.

____

2. Mischa said that she didn't enjoy the film.

____

3. Joel admitted that he left the door open.

____

4. Franz whispered that he hadn't done anything wrong.

____

5. He explained that the class had been cancelled.

____

Hint: Remember to add the right punctuation inside the inverted commas.

/ 5

Colons

Add a colon to complete each sentence. For example:

Hans only cared about one person**:** himself.

6. Before you start, gather your equipment a bowl, icing sugar and a spatula.
7. The snowboarders were miserable for a reason no snow.
8. It's easy to operate press this button and you will start the engine.
9. I love three things in life my friends, my family and my dog.
10. It was an obvious issue Xiu hated swimming in the sea.
11. The café is not difficult to find go down this corridor and then turn left.
12. I vote that we support one charity this year the R.S.P.C.A..
13. Romesh had one dream he wanted to travel the world.

/ 8

Mixed Punctuation Questions

Each of these sentences contains one punctuation error. Rewrite the sentence correctly underneath. For example:

Kevin and I went to the shop's to buy sweets.
Kevin and I went to the shops to buy sweets.

1. "I think it's time you went to bed", said Mum.

____

2. Theres nothing in the fridge (except ham).

____

3. "When can we go to the cinema," whined Billy.

____

4. Megan searched up and, down the street for the baby's rattle.

____

5. The old mens' cars weren't parked outside.

____

/5

Each of these sentences is missing one punctuation mark. Add the missing punctuation mark to each of the sentences. For example:

" Hi Jack , " said Ajit.

6. My grandpa , who is 80 this month still plays badminton every week .
7. " Which of these drawings is yours , Anthony " asked Mrs Phillips .
8. I'd like to thank three people Beth , Amy and Eshana .
9. Karl bought a jumper , a jacket and a hat when we went shopping
10. " It's not fair ! I want to stay up late too , complained Suzie .
11. My parents have old-fashioned names they're called Phyllis and Neville .
12. I buy sweets lemon sherbets) after my swimming lessons .
13. " Calm down boys . You're getting over-excited " scolded Mum .

/8

Mixed Punctuation Questions

The following short passages have no punctuation. Rewrite the passages with no mistakes. Each passage has 10 missing punctuation marks.

1. camilla looked around the park but she could not see the ladys puppy anywhere she wanted to find it because the woman had been so upset rollo she called

/ 10

Hint: Circle places in the passage where you think there is a mistake before you start writing it out again.

2. the annual village fair will take place in greenbridge tomorrow afternoon jasper dupree the famous chef will be giving demonstrations get there early

/ 10

Plurals

Plurals

Write the correct plural of the word in brackets. For example:

She loves riding ___ponies___ **(pony)**.

1. We had crunchy roast ___________ **(potato)** with our Sunday lunch.
2. There were no ___________ **(witness)** to the theft of the pocket watch.
3. The ___________ **(leaf)** on the trees turn crimson and gold in autumn.
4. We saw the family of ___________ **(fox)** who live at the bottom of our garden.
5. I've had three pet ___________ **(canary)**; the most recent one's called Boris.
6. Anouk is taking salmon ___________ **(sandwich)** in her packed lunch.
7. My cousins consume six ___________ **(loaf)** of bread every week.
8. I'm playing ___________ **(domino)** in a tournament on Tuesday night.

/ 8

Plurals

Write the correct plural of the word in brackets. For example:

The theatre was crammed with noisy ___children___ **(child)**.

Hint: Say the plural word out loud to check that it sounds right.

9. The dentist declared that Susie's ___________ **(tooth)** were healthy.
10. In Victorian times, only ___________ **(man)** were allowed to vote.
11. We simply couldn't squeeze any more ___________ **(person)** onto the train.
12. Sunesh was woken by the sound of the angry ___________ **(goose)** honking in the yard.
13. Hygiene was so poor in the Middle Ages that many peasants had ___________ **(louse)**.
14. Marco's ___________ **(foot)** were aching after the gruelling mountain walk.
15. Stewart's grandmother loved growing exotic ___________ **(cactus)**.
16. We were chased by a flock of ___________ **(sheep)** when we went for a picnic.

/ 8

Homophones

Homophones

Choose the correct homophone from the brackets. For example:

I have curly brown <u>hair</u> **(hare hair)**.

1. We're having __________ **(our hour)** garage converted into a giant ball pool.
2. Her new bike had a __________ **(steal steel)** frame so it was quite heavy.
3. Meredith had a new perfume which had an unusual __________ **(sent scent)**.
4. I used too much __________ **(flour flower)** so my cake failed to rise.
5. These big cartons of milk are very hard to __________ **(poor pour)**.
6. We sat on the dock and watched the boats __________ **(sail sale)** past.
7. When Keiko wore shorts, her __________ **(bear bare)** legs were bitten by mosquitoes.
8. Jon didn't have enough money for his bus __________ **(fair fare)**.
9. We took the wrong __________ **(root route)**, despite looking at the map.
10. The CD wasn't working; it had __________ **(warn worn)** out over time.

/ 10

Homophones

Complete each sentence using **there**, **their** or **they're**. For example:

We're going to <u>their</u> house for Christmas.

11. Jakub is anxious about meeting my family, but __________ quite conventional really.
12. Chi was desperate to see __________ new ferret.

13. We play lacrosse on that pitch over __________.
14. When my dad was young, __________ was a huge reservoir here.
15. Polar bears clean __________ fur by rolling in the snow.
16. I don't know why __________ playing that terrible song.

/ 6

Prefixes and Suffixes

Prefixes

Add the prefix **in**, **im** or **il** to make each word negative. For example:

These maths questions are __im__possible.

1. Katrin lost the debate because her argument was completely _____logical.
2. My little brother is really _____mature; he finds burping hilarious.
3. The con man was convicted of all sorts of _____legal activities.
4. The lead actor in the film was _____capable of stringing a sentence together.
5. Heidi knew her sketch was _____perfect, but she just couldn't get Dinah's nose right.
6. My sister spent an hour in the bathroom this morning; she's so _____considerate.
7. The rabbit enjoyed the novel, even though the plot was totally _____plausible.
8. Kazuo would have got a better mark, but his writing is _____legible.

/ 8

Suffixes

Add the suffix **ment**, **ful** or **ness** to complete the word in brackets.
For example:

The lake was always so __peaceful__ **(peace)** at dawn.

9. Cathy was planning to travel around the world during her ____________ **(retire)**.
10. Gulnar asked for Darren's ____________ **(forgive)** when she broke his favourite mug.
11. The toolset was very ____________ **(use)**, but Kay wished they'd bought her a dog instead.
12. She received outstanding ____________ **(treat)** during her illness.
13. Chandra gave up his chair out of ____________ **(polite)**.
14. The chefs reached an ____________ **(agree)** about who was in charge of dessert.
15. We couldn't help but join in the ____________ **(merry)**.
16. Nina's ____________ **(beauty)** new dress had glue all down the front.

Hint: The spelling of the word may change when a suffix is added.

/ 8

Awkward Spellings

Vowels

Add either **ie** or **ei** to form the words correctly. For example:

The path across the f__ie__ld was really muddy.

1. The jewel th_____f had stolen Lady Bunting's priceless diamond necklace.
2. The pr_____st came into school to talk to us about the harvest festival.
3. Kit asked for a rec_____pt in case his mum didn't like the tarantula he'd bought her.
4. Mrs Sharma's f_____rce dog barks at me every time I walk past her house.
5. Tiago asked for an extra large p_____ce of cake.
6. I don't like bubble baths and n_____ther does my cat.
7. The children were rel_____ved when they reached their destination.
8. I p_____rced the juice carton with the end of the straw.

Hint: Remember the rule: 'i before e, except after c (but only when it rhymes with bee)'.

/ 8

Consonants

Complete these words with the correct single or double consonant. For example:

The ra__bb__it scampered back to its burrow.

9. Art is brilliant, but my favourite lesson is hi_____tory.
10. Meera wasn't a_____owed sweets, except on special occasions.
11. When Paul gave Sara his a_____ress, he really hoped that she'd write.
12. We're jetting off on our holiday to Costa Rica to_____orrow!
13. Kell a_____epted Mo's apology for the mud-throwing incident.
14. The walrus wondered if it was really ne_____essary to wear the wetsuit Mum had bought him.
15. Stop what you're doing imme_____iately if the fire alarm goes off.
16. Sophie finally su_____eeded in her quest to ban cabbage from school meals.

/ 8

Mixed Spelling Questions

Each sentence contains a spelling mistake. Underline the word with the error and write the correct spelling on the line. For example:

The chef grabbed his knifes and started chopping. knives

Hint: If you can't spot the mistake straight away, look carefully at letter combinations that are often misspelt, such as double letters and plurals.

1. Hanna loved going to the field to feed the donkies. ________
2. Mary made a meringue filled with cream and raspberrys. ________
3. Miyako was startled by the sudden nock at the door. ________
4. Sam wasn't sure which starecase led to the basement. ________
5. Tiddles edged away from the empty fish tank, looking gilty. ________
6. Parvani thought a ham and honey sanwich would be delicious. ________

/ 6

7. I thought the film was excellent; I'd definitely reccommend it. ________
8. Marta's parents were very proud of there clever daughter. ________
9. Remember to wiegh your ingredients when you're baking. ________
10. The son was shining so we relaxed on the outdoor terrace. ________
11. Our annual holiday in Cornwall was wonderfull. ________
12. Paolo practised regularly ahead of the piano compitition. ________

/ 6

13. Vegetarians get protien from foods such as lentils or beans. ________
14. He didn't actualy like jam tarts, but it seemed polite to eat one. ________
15. Ian found that hopping was a very imefficient way to travel. ________
16. Eric had a fine collectian of novelty paper clips. ________
17. They were bursting with excitment before they went skiing. ________
18. The secratary was annoyed that she didn't have her own office. ________

/ 6

Mixed Spelling Questions

Underline the correct word to complete each sentence. For example:

I went to the shop to **(buy by)** some milk.

1. **(To Too)** many people, Kate was an excellent role model.
2. The puppy got **(to too)** excited and knocked over the precious statue.
3. I don't know **(whether weather)** to go for a bike ride today.
4. The zombie wanted to go hiking, but the **(whether weather)** forecast wasn't very good.
5. "Please may I **(lend borrow)** your protractor?" asked Hamsa.
6. "Only if you **(lend borrow)** me your green pen," answered Rhiannon.

/ 6

7. I couldn't **(where wear)** my football shirt because it was covered in mud.
8. Jamelia suddenly remembered **(where wear)** she had left her keys.
9. There's nothing **(worse worst)** than sandy food at the beach.
10. I am the **(worse worst)** snooker player in the entire family.
11. Max thought he had done **(well good)** in his saxophone exam.
12. Chunni was **(well good)** at making new friends, so she had a busy social life.

/ 6

13. I was devastated to **(loose lose)** the cross-country race.
14. I forgot to wear socks so my shoes were very **(loose lose)**.
15. I'm extremely full but I've got a craving for the lemon **(desert dessert)**.
16. He had wandered for days through the barren **(desert dessert)** with no water.
17. That's the man **(which who)** tried to sell me a luminous inflatable pinboard.
18. I bought two polka-dot shirts, **(which who)** used up all my pocket money.

/ 6

Alliteration and Onomatopoeia

Alliteration

Underline all of the words that form the alliteration. For example:

The silly spider spun a strangely slippery web.

1. Tom has the most terrible temper; he's a ticking time bomb.
2. I licked my luscious lemon lolly until there was a little left.
3. Bernard the bumbling bear knocked over the blue bucket.
4. Darshan dreaded dustbin day: the dustmen disturbed him at dawn.
5. The creepy caretaker crunched on a bowl of cereal.
6. Fiona folded the faded photo and fixed it to the front of the file.
7. Naughty Naseem tied a knot in Mrs Knight's new laces.
8. The cheeky chimp chased a cart loaded with chocolate bars.

Hint: Watch out for words that begin with the same letter but are pronounced differently, like 'game' and 'giant'.

/ 8

Onomatopoeia

Use an onomatopoeic word to complete each sentence. For example:

Ed ate the crisp with a loud ___crunch___ .

9. The stone made a loud ______________ as it landed in the flowing river.
10. The fly ______________ past my left ear.
11. The branch of the old tree ______________ in the wind.
12. In the woodland you can hear the owls ______________ at night.
13. The kitchen tap was broken and water ______________ into the sink all day.
14. The frog ______________ quietly as it sat on the lily pad.
15. I love the smell of sausages ______________ in the pan.
16. Lenny fell out of bed with a ______________.

/ 8

Imagery

Imagery

Each sentence contains a metaphor, simile or personification.
Write down the technique used in each sentence. For example:

Libby's eyes were as blue as the sea. simile

1. Pam's dog's growl was a low rumble of thunder. ____________
2. The wind shouted angrily across the lonely moor. ____________
3. The dancer moved as gracefully as a wounded hippo. ____________
4. Jonah's nose was an icicle clinging to his face. ____________
5. The tulip field shimmered in the sun like a carpet of jewels. ____________
6. Gran's kettle whistled joyfully that it was time for tea. ____________
7. The desert was a burning sea of sandy waves. ____________
8. Our cat's tongue was as rough as sandpaper. ____________

/ 8

Imagery

Complete these similes and metaphors using a suitable word.
For example:

The old man was as bald as a boiled egg.

9. The moon was as bright as ____________.
10. Her cheek was as cold and smooth as ____________.
11. The rabbit stood perfectly still; he was a ____________.
12. Moira's voice was as beautiful as ____________.
13. When Mr Duggan was angry, he was a ____________.
14. Alia dashed madly home, her arms flapping like ____________.
15. The rock pool bustled with life, like a ____________.
16. The lake was clear and still; it was a ____________.

Hint: Don't go for obvious comparisons — be as inventive as you can.

/ 8

Abbreviations

Abbreviations

Write down the full word for the abbreviation in bold.
For example:

Padma loved riding her **bike**. bicycle

1. I bought some sausages after seeing the **ad**. ______
2. Mrs McCrone set us extra **maths** homework. ______
3. I like to watch cartoons on **telly** after dinner. ______
4. Carly took a fabulous **photo** with her new camera. ______
5. I went to see **Dr** Godfrey when I had chickenpox. ______
6. We travelled by **plane** when we went to Italy. ______
7. Dan bought a **paper** to read about current events. ______
8. Professor Scattley was conducting experiments in her **lab**. ______

/ 8

Hint: If you're not sure how to spell a word, check your answer in the dictionary.

Abbreviations

Write down the most common abbreviation of the word in bold.
For example:

We talked on the **telephone**. phone

9. The **hippopotamus** wallowed in a warm mud bath. ______
10. Yusef put his freshly made trifle in the **refrigerator**. ______
11. A fully grown **rhinoceros** has escaped from Hilton Zoo. ______
12. Chandra couldn't wait for the **examination** to be over. ______
13. My pet mouse goes to the **gymnasium** every day. ______
14. Mrs Brookes read the **quotation** with interest. ______
15. We took our cat, Mr Whiskers, to the **veterinarian**. ______
16. Joyce was off school after a nasty bout of **influenza**. ______

/ 8

Synonyms and Antonyms

Synonyms

Underline the word from the brackets that is the best synonym for the word in bold as it is used in the sentence. For example:

The castle was very **creepy**. **(sneaky mysterious spooky)**

Hint: Read all of the options carefully before you underline your answer.

1. We looked around the **majestic** manor house. **(impressive spacious monstrous)**
2. Bernie loved playing **pranks** on his sister. **(riddles tricks mischief)**
3. Jenny felt very **relaxed** after her bubble bath. **(drowsy carefree warm)**
4. Karrie was **anxious** about going on the roller coaster. **(nervous excited angry)**
5. People were **disgusted** by Phil Smith's behaviour. **(surprised bothered revolted)**
6. The head teacher looked fierce but she was actually very **amiable**. **(friendly caring generous)**
7. Hari jumped when he heard the eerie **moan**. **(grumble groan weeping)**
8. Police successfully captured the **ruthless** burglar. **(evil savage cruel)**

/ 8

Antonyms

Underline the word from the brackets that is the best antonym for the word in bold as it is used in the sentence. For example:

Jan felt **proud** of his painting. **(pleased ashamed bored)**

9. Heulwen made a **generous** donation to the charity. **(noble greedy stingy)**
10. Red squirrels are increasingly **rare** in the UK. **(common normal scarce)**
11. Mia's new camera was very **compact**. **(bulky condensed sophisticated)**
12. Francesca's new flat was really **luxurious**. **(cold basic unpleasant)**
13. Scruffy felt quite **neglected** when the new puppy arrived. **(pleased abandoned cherished)**
14. Louis **alarmed** his dad by leaping up in the middle of dinner. **(reassured terrified impressed)**
15. Pascal **scowled** when he wasn't allowed to leave. **(frowned grinned smirked)**
16. Following a short delay, normal service will **resume**. **(start delay cease)**

/ 8

Spotting and Understanding Devices

Read the passage below, then answer the questions that follow.

Hester crept through the dense undergrowth, signalling to Benito, her cameraman, to remain silent. To Hester, the forest was a treasure chest of filming opportunities; she just hoped that today would be a good day. She cursed softly as thorny vines gleefully tangled themselves in her mop of curly blonde hair. Parting the emerald green fronds of the fragrant ferns, Hester gasped. A few metres away from her was a whole family of chimps!

Making sure that Benito was recording, she turned breathlessly to face the camera. Its red light was a friendly eye, winking to show that all was well. She was as excited as a child at Christmas, and couldn't believe her luck.

"This is a rare sight," she said quietly to the camera. "As you can see, the large male is cracking the hard outer shells of nuts. Meanwhile, the female is grooming her infant, cradling him carefully in her hands."

Hint: Read the text carefully before you start to answer the questions — it'll be easier to find the answers if you know what happens when.

Write down which technique is used in the following:

1. "the forest was a treasure chest of filming opportunities". (line 2) ____________
2. "as excited as a child at Christmas". (lines 7-8) ____________
3. "thorny vines gleefully tangled themselves". (lines 3-4) ____________

Find an example from the text of the following:

4. alliteration. ____________________________
5. onomatopoeia. ____________________________
6. an abbreviation. ____________
7. a synonym of 'thick'. ____________
8. an antonym of 'typical'. ____________

/ 8

Spotting and Understanding Devices

Read the passage below, then answer the questions that follow.
Underline the correct option for each question.

Haji woke with a start. The curtains whispered in the breeze and when he peered out from under the dark cave of his duvet, he could see two dimly glowing lights hovering beneath his desk.

"Khalid," he hissed, "are you awake?"

There was a groan from the other side of the room as his twin brother stirred.

"Go back to sleep, Haji," he mumbled groggily. "It's just a nightmare." Within seconds he was quietly snoring again.

Haji, however, couldn't fall asleep so easily. The pair of lights seemed to be getting closer and he could make out a low rumble, like the growl of a strange animal. He suddenly felt very scared; his heartbeat was a drum thumping inside his chest.

Hint: Think about how the text makes you feel to help you answer these questions.

1. The author says that Haji's duvet is a "cave" (line 2). This shows that his duvet is:

   A shaped like a cave. **B** made of rock. **C** very cold and dark.

2. The author says that Haji "hissed" (line 4). Why do you think Haji does this?

   A He's angry. **B** He's in pain. **C** He doesn't want to make much noise.

3. The author says that Haji's heartbeat was a "drum thumping inside his chest" (line 10). This shows that:

   A his heartbeat was loud. **B** he was playing the drums. **C** his heartbeat was quiet.

4. "The curtains whispered in the breeze" (line 1). What does this tell you about how the curtains moved?

   A They moved softly. **B** They moved quickly. **C** They moved constantly.

5. The author compares the noise Haji hears to the "growl of a strange animal" (line 9). What does this suggest about whatever is making the noise?

   A It's dangerous. **B** It's friendly. **C** It's sleeping.

/ 5

Writing Fiction

Adjectives

Replace the word in bold with a different adjective. For example:

The flowers smelt **nice**. delightful

1. Calvin was **tired** after staying up all night. ____________
2. We bought a **large** bag of popcorn. ____________
3. The shopping centre was **busy** on Saturday. ____________
4. Petra found the scientific article **boring**. ____________
5. Basma told a **funny** joke about poodles. ____________
6. Our maths homework was really **hard**. ____________
7. The new girl in our class is **small**. ____________
8. Siân's new car was already **dirty** when she got home. ____________

/ 8

Clauses

Add a clause to complete these sentences. For example:

Jon fell over because his shoelaces were undone.

Hint: A clause is part of a sentence — it has to have a verb.

9. Chen ran to the shop ____________________
10. Maggie owns a dog ____________________
11. Danny was really happy ____________________
12. I used to like horses ____________________
13. We drove to the beach ____________________
14. Shima read a book ____________________
15. Arjun was angry ____________________
16. We're going on holiday ____________________

/ 8

Writing Fiction

Adjectives

Adjectives make your stories more detailed. Write three adjectives to describe these characters and settings. For example:

An artist ___kind___ ___beautiful___ ___imaginative___

Hint: Think about each character's appearance and personality.

1. A witch ________ ________ ________
2. A forest ________ ________ ________
3. A policeman ________ ________ ________
4. A city ________ ________ ________
5. A lamb ________ ________ ________
6. A field ________ ________ ________

/ 6

Planning

For each of the titles below, choose one of the characters and settings you wrote about above. Write a sentence about what will happen at the beginning, the middle and the end of the story.

7. **"An Exciting Day Out"**

Beginning: ________________

Middle: ________________

End: ________________

/ 3

8. **"A Surprising Adventure"**

Beginning: ________________

Middle: ________________

End: ________________

/ 3

9. **Choose one of your plans and write a full story of about 250 words.**

Writing Non-Fiction

You can improve your writing by understanding the purpose of different texts. Write down whether each of these sentences is describing (D), persuading (P) or informing (I). For example:

Help the environment by recycling your drinks cans. P

1. Canada Geese migrate thousands of miles south each year. ____
2. Can you afford to miss out on six months of free gym membership? ____
3. The Great Wall of China stretches over more than 5000 miles. ____
4. The remote wood was filled with the enchanting sound of birdsong. ____
5. Please give generously; these children desperately need your help. ____
6. The cherry tree's branches swayed gently and tiny petals drifted down. ____

/ 6

Hint: Remember, if the text is trying to get the reader to do something, it's persuasive.

Write a plan for these essays. Include an introduction, two points for the middle and a point for your conclusion.

7. **Describe a famous person you admire.**

Beginning: ____

Middle 1: ____

2: ____

End: ____

/ 4

8. **Are children given too much homework?**

Beginning: ____

Middle 1: ____

2: ____

End: ____

/ 4

Writing Non-Fiction

Write a sentence arguing **for** and **against** these statements.
For example:

Children should learn a foreign language at school.

For: It's easier to learn a language when you're young.

Against: There'll be less time for maths and English.

1. **Children under sixteen should travel on buses for free.**

   For: ____________________

   Against: ____________________

2. **Children should not have to do sport at school.**

   For: ____________________

   Against: ____________________

3. **Every town should have a library.**

   For: ____________________

   Against: ____________________

4. **Keeping animals in zoos should be illegal.**

   For: ____________________

   Against: ____________________

/ 8

Write a plan for each of these essay titles. Then turn your plan into a full answer. Write about 250 words for each.

Hint: You can make up facts to make your arguments more convincing.

5. Write a letter to a friend persuading them to visit you.
6. Write a magazine article describing your perfect day.
7. Write a letter to a friend telling them what your bedroom is like.
8. Write an essay to be put into a time capsule, informing people what modern life is like.

Assessment Test 1

This section contains six practice tests, which get progressively harder.
Allow 40 minutes to do each test and work as quickly and as carefully as you can.

If you want to attempt each test more than once, you will need to print **multiple-choice answer sheets** for these questions from our website — go to cgpbooks.co.uk/11plus/answer-sheets. If you'd prefer to answer the questions on the page, just follow the instructions in the question.

Read this passage carefully and answer the questions that follow.

Pet Rocks

Have you ever wanted a pet, but been put off by the work needed to take care of it? In 1975, one entrepreneur set about trying to find a solution for this problem. This individual was Gary Dahl, an advertising executive from California, who came up with the unique idea of keeping rocks as pets.

Dahl decided that a rock was an ideal pet because it didn't need feeding, walking or bathing, and there weren't any expensive vet bills to worry about. Certain that Pet Rocks could make his fortune, Dahl started to sell his Rocks to the public.

Over the next year, Dahl sold more than a million Pet Rocks at $3.95 each. Each Rock came with a carrying case complete with air holes and a bed of straw for the Rock's comfort, as well as a thirty-two page instruction manual on how to look after it. These manuals included tips on how to train the Rocks to sit, stay and even roll over (with a bit of help from their owner).

Pet Rocks sold well during the Christmas period, but they were destined to be a fad. Despite Dahl's best efforts they soon became a thing of the past and, after 1975, sales dried up. Fortunately for Dahl, he had already made his fortune.

Nowadays Dahl runs his own advertising company, but he remains an inspiration to many modern inventors. The Pet Rocks phenomenon has inspired numerous other creators to think of new crazes that could also sweep the world and make millions of dollars.

Answer these questions about the text that you've just read.
Circle the letter that matches the correct answer.

1. What job did Gary Dahl have before he started selling Pet Rocks?

A He ran an advertising company.
B He was an entrepreneur.
C He worked in marketing.
D He worked in advertising.
E He was a salesman.

2. Which of these statements is not true?

A Gary Dahl lived in California.
B Pet Rocks stopped selling in 1975.
C The Rocks came in a carrying case.
D Rocks sold best over Christmas.
E The instruction manual said Rocks could be trained to roll over.

/ 2

3. According to the passage, why did Dahl believe that Rocks were the perfect pet?

   1 They are house trained.
   2 They come with an instruction manual.
   3 They don't need exercise.
   4 They don't need veterinary treatment.
   5 They only need bathing once a week.

   A 1 and 2
   B 2 and 3
   C 2 and 5
   D 3 and 4
   E 4 and 5

4. According to the passage, which of these wasn't mentioned in the instruction manual?

   A How to teach the Rock to sit.
   B How to teach the Rock to roll over.
   C How to care for your Rock.
   D How to teach the Rock to stay.
   E How to make a bed of straw for your Rock.

5. When were Pet Rocks most successful?

   A After 1975
   B The beginning of 1975
   C December 1975
   D February 1976
   E Christmas 1976

6. Why did Pet Rocks stop selling?

   A They were illegal.
   B Dahl ran out of rocks.
   C They were old-fashioned.
   D People lost interest in them.
   E They were too expensive.

7. Why is Gary Dahl inspiring?

   A He is an executive.
   B He runs his own advertising company.
   C He invented the perfect pet.
   D He is rich.
   E He showed that anyone can be successful with the right idea.

/ 5

Carry on to the next question →→

Answer these questions about the way words and phrases are used in the passage.

8. Which of these words is closest in meaning to "unique" (line 3)?

A Unusual
B Profitable
C Original
D Disastrous
E Amusing

9. Which of these is closest in meaning to "fad" (line 11)?

A Christmas gift
B Short-lived trend
C Bad idea
D Treasured possession
E Top-seller

10. Explain the meaning of the phrase "sales dried up" (line 12) as it is used in the passage.

A People stopped buying Pet Rocks.
B Pet Rocks stopped being profitable.
C Pet Rocks were hard to find in the shops.
D Shops stopped stocking Pet Rocks.
E Customers thought buying Pet Rocks was a waste of money.

11. "Dahl sold more than a million Pet Rocks" (line 7).
Which of these words is a verb?

A Dahl
B sold
C more
D million
E Pet

12. "solution" (line 2) and "phenomenon" (line 15) are examples of which part of speech?

A Adjectives
B Metaphors
C Verbs
D Adverbs
E Nouns

/ 5

Read this poem carefully and answer the questions that follow.

An adapted extract from 'The Quangle Wangle's Hat'

On the top of the Crumpetty Tree
The Quangle Wangle sat,
But his face you could not see,
On account of his Beaver Hat.
For his Hat was a hundred and two feet wide,
With ribbons and bibbons on every side,
And bells, and buttons, and loops, and lace,
So that nobody ever could see the face
Of the Quangle Wangle Quee.

The Quangle Wangle said
To himself on the Crumpetty Tree,
"Jam, and jelly, and bread
Are the best food for me!
But the longer I live on this Crumpetty Tree
The plainer that ever it seems to me
That very few people come this way
And that life on the whole is far from great!"
Said the Quangle Wangle Quee.

But there came to the Crumpetty Tree
Mr. and Mrs. Canary;
And they said, "Did ever you see
Any spot so charmingly airy?
May we build a nest on your lovely Hat?
Mr. Quangle Wangle, grant us that!
O please let us come and build a nest
Of whatever material suits you best,
Mr. Quangle Wangle Quee!"

And besides, to the Crumpetty Tree
Came the Stork, the Duck, and the Owl;
The Snail and the Bumble-Bee,
The Frog and the Fimble Fowl
(The Fimble Fowl, with a Corkscrew leg);
And all of them said, "We humbly beg
We may build our homes on your lovely Hat,
Mr. Quangle Wangle, grant us that!
Mr. Quangle Wangle Quee!"

And the Quangle Wangle said
To himself on the Crumpetty Tree,
"When all these creatures move
What a wonderful noise there'll be!"
And at night by the light of the Mulberry moon
They danced to the flute of the Blue Baboon,
On the broad green leaves of the Crumpetty Tree,
And all were as happy as happy could be,
With the Quangle Wangle Quee.

by Edward Lear

Answer these questions about the text that you've just read.
Circle the letter that matches the correct answer.

13. Why can't you tell what the Quangle Wangle looks like?

A He sits at the top of a tall tree.
B He wears a big hat.
C He is shy and hides his face.
D He is too tall.
E There is a nest in front of his face.

/ 1

Carry on to the next question → →

14. How does the Quangle Wangle feel in the second verse?

A Carefree
B Hungry
C Lonely
D Merry
E Content

15. Who came to the tree first?

A Two birds
B Nobody knows
C One bird
D A frog
E A bumble bee

16. Which of the following is not mentioned in the poem?

A A duck
B A baboon
C An owl
D A stork
E A heron

17. Why do visitors come to see the Quangle Wangle?

A To see the Crumpetty Tree
B To make noise with the Quangle Wangle
C To live on the Quangle Wangle's hat
D To dance with the Quangle Wangle
E To build a nest for the Quangle Wangle

18. How does the Quangle Wangle feel about the visitors?

A Confused
B Daunted
C Uncertain
D Delighted
E Angry

19. What type of poem is 'The Quangle Wangle's Hat'?

A A limerick
B A fable
C A sonnet
D A shape poem
E A nonsense poem

/ 6

Answer these questions about the way words and phrases are used in the poem.

20. What could the phrase "On account of" (line 4) most accurately be replaced by?

A Given that
B In spite of
C Because of
D Instead of
E As well as

21. What could the word "airy" (line 22) most accurately be replaced by?

A Open
B Light
C Windy
D Beautiful
E Outdoors

22. Which of these is closest in meaning to "grant" (line 24)?

A Reward
B Refuse
C Tell
D Allow
E Show

23. "The Frog and the Fimble Fowl" (line 31) is an example of:

A alliteration.
B rhyme.
C a simile.
D a metaphor.
E personification.

24. What type of word is "humbly" (line 33)?

A Adjective
B Adverb
C Noun
D Verb
E Pronoun

/ 5

Carry on to the next question → →

In this passage, there are some spelling mistakes. Circle the letter which matches the part of the sentence with the mistake. If there's no mistake, circle N.

25. Suntime Foods wishes to announse a new breakfast product designed for young families.

A	B	C	D	N

26. Containing a range of delicious and nutritious ingrediants, it's tasty, crunchy, colourful

A	B	C	D	N

27. and guaranteed to be a breakfast serial of exceptional quality. Our farmers harvest their

A	B	C	D	N

28. organic crops with extra care to ensure perfect freshness every time. It's delightfull with

A	B	C	D	N

29. or without a splash of chilled milk, so why not start your day with a bowl of "Oat Pops"?

A	B	C	D	N

/ 5

In this passage, there are some punctuation mistakes. Circle the letter which matches the part of the sentence with the mistake. If there's no mistake, circle N.

30. Gripping tightly to the rope: both boys shuffled forward so slowly that they barely moved.

A	B	C	D	N

31. The water was freezing, causing them to shiver almost uncontrollably. Javed felt it pulling

A	B	C	D	N

32. vigorously at his ankles. As they approached the island in the centre of the River dee, Lewis

A	B	C	D	N

33. turned and called, "This is no fun, is it? but his voice was carried away on the breeze. Tears

A	B	C	D	N

34. streaming down his face and lips quivering he clenched his teeth bravely and struggled on.

A	B	C	D	N

/ 5

Choose the right word or phrase to fill the gap. Circle the letter which matches the correct word.

35. Natalie **was were is did had** watching the front door with eager anticipation. She had
A B C D E

36. **be being been was did** given some wonderful presents for her birthday, but she was waiting
A B C D E

37. **of at to for on** the postman to deliver her cards. She hoped that her favourite uncle
A B C D E

38. had remembered to send her a birthday card all the way **to in for of from** New Zealand.
A B C D E

39. Natalie tapped her fingers impatiently. When **must may can could would** the postman come?
A B C D E

40. Then her mum, **what who how which that** was in the kitchen, heard an excited yell!
A B C D E

/ 6

Total / 40

End of Test

Assessment Test 2

Allow 40 minutes to do this test and work as quickly and as carefully as you can.

You can print **multiple-choice answer sheets** for these questions from our website — go to cgpbooks.co.uk/11plus/answer-sheets. If you'd prefer to answer them on the page, just follow the instructions in the question.

Read this passage carefully and answer the questions that follow.

The Treasure Hunt

Jimmy looked with increasing frustration from the card in his clammy hand to his friends' bewildered faces. He read the clue aloud, for what felt like the hundredth time:

"Head west to find the final clue,
If you cooperate you won't feel blue,
No fowl play, be fair and right,
And the treasure could be yours tonight."

"We may as well accept defeat in this treasure hunt, Jimmy," whispered Felicity.

Jimmy felt a wave of disappointment crash over him. It was the final evening of Park Hill School's annual camping trip, taking place as usual in the woods surrounding Westbury Farm, and winning the treasure hunt with his best friends would be the perfect way to end the weekend. Jimmy had loved every minute of it: the nature walks, building dens, listening to ghost stories around the campfire and, above all, sleeping outdoors, listening to the strange rustlings of the countryside at night.

Up until this point, they had managed to work out each clue quite swiftly and only Freddie Farley's team was keeping up with them. Freddie, the school football captain, was infamous for being a bad loser and wasn't above using underhand tactics to try and win. Jimmy suspected Freddie was responsible for their broken compass and missing map.

"We are not giving up." Jimmy spoke weakly.

"Perhaps 'west' means 'Westbury Farm'?" suggested Felicity, tentatively.

Jimmy's team turned as one to look at the farm. It seemed as though 'coop' and 'fowl' might unravel this maddening mystery.

Answer these questions about the text that you've just read.
Circle the letter that matches the correct answer.

1. Why were Jimmy's friends "bewildered" (line 2)?

   A They were lost in the woods.
   B They were finding the treasure hunt difficult.
   C They did not understand why Jimmy wanted to win.
   D They were bored because Jimmy kept talking.
   E They were confused by the clue.

2. Why did Jimmy feel as though he had read the clue a hundred times?

   A He had already read it 99 times.
   B He was finding the clue hard to read.
   C He had read the clue lots of times but his team could not solve it.
   D He had read the clue lots of times but his team were not interested.
   E He enjoyed reading the clue so he kept reading it aloud.

/ 2

3. Why did Jimmy speak "weakly" (line 17)?

A He had lost his voice because he had been talking so much.
B He did not really believe what he was saying.
C He was speaking quietly so Freddie wouldn't overhear.
D He was tired so he couldn't speak loudly.
E He was annoyed because Felicity wanted to give up.

4. How often did the school camping trip take place?

A Once a month
B Every six months
C Once a year
D Occasionally
E The text doesn't say

5. Which of the following activities is not mentioned in the text?

A Building campfires
B Sleeping outdoors
C Nature walks
D Building dens
E Listening to ghost stories

6. Why was Freddie "infamous" (line 14)?

A He was the school football captain.
B He was using underhand tactics.
C He couldn't stand it if he didn't win.
D He was the most popular boy at school.
E He had broken Jimmy's team's compass and taken their map.

7. How do you think Jimmy's team feels in lines 19-20?

A Nervous
B Confused
C Hopeful
D Confident
E Thoughtful

/ 5

Carry on to the next question →→

Answer these questions about the way words and phrases are used in the passage.

8. Which of these words is closest in meaning to "frustration" (line 1)?

A Annoyance
B Disappointment
C Worry
D Fear
E Shame

9. Which of these is closest in meaning to "underhand" (line 15)?

A Tricky
B Clever
C Imaginative
D Dishonest
E Secret

10. The word "tentatively" (line 18) could most accurately be replaced by:

A casually.
B quietly.
C slowly.
D hopefully.
E uncertainly.

11. What are the words "maddening mystery" (line 20) an example of?

A A simile
B Alliteration
C A rhyme
D Personification
E A metaphor

12. "Jimmy felt a wave of disappointment crash over him" (line 8).
What is this an example of?

A A proverb
B Personification
C A simile
D A metaphor
E Alliteration

/ 5

Read this poem carefully and answer the questions that follow.

An extract from 'The Spider and the Fly'

"Will you walk into my parlour?" said the spider to the fly;
" 'Tis the prettiest little parlour that ever you did spy.
The way into my parlour is up a winding stair,
And I have many curious things to shew when you are there."
"Oh no, no," said the little fly; "to ask me is in vain,
For who goes up your winding stair can ne'er come down again."

"I'm sure you must be weary, dear, with soaring up so high.
Will you rest upon my little bed?" said the spider to the fly.
"There are pretty curtains drawn around; the sheets are fine and thin,
And if you like to rest awhile, I'll snugly tuck you in!"
"Oh no, no," said the little fly, "for I've often heard it said,
They never, never wake again who sleep upon your bed!"

"Sweet creature!" said the spider, "you're witty and you're wise;
How handsome are your gauzy wings; how brilliant are your eyes!
I have a little looking-glass upon my parlour shelf;
If you'll step in one moment, dear, you shall behold yourself."
"I thank you, gentle sir," she said, "for what you're pleased to say,
And, bidding you good morning now, I'll call another day."

by Mary Howitt

Answer these questions about the text that you've just read.
Circle the letter that matches the correct answer.

13. How does the spider try to get the fly into his parlour in the first verse?

A By tempting the fly
B By flattering the fly
C By threatening the fly
D By upsetting the fly
E By teasing the fly

14. Which of the following does the spider claim to have in his parlour?

A A bed with a warm quilt
B Interesting objects
C A winding staircase
D Glass ornaments
E Attractive curtains over the windows

/ 2

Carry on to the next question → →

15. Why does the fly turn down the spider's offer?

A She doesn't want to climb the staircase.
B She is not interested in seeing the spider's parlour.
C She is too vain to accept the offer.
D She would rather soar up high in the sky.
E She thinks she will never escape from the parlour.

16. Why does the spider say that the fly might need to lie on the bed?

A She will be tired from walking up the stairs.
B The bed is very comfortable.
C She will need to rest after looking at the curious things.
D She is tired from all her flying.
E The spider loves having visitors to stay.

17. How would you describe the fly's attitude towards the spider?

A Irritated
B Curious
C Distrustful
D Grateful
E Angry

18. In the third verse, what does the spider promise to show the fly?

A What she looks like
B A looking glass
C The parlour shelf
D Some pretty curtains
E A pair of spectacles

19. The language used by the spider in the third verse could best be described as:

A polite.
B kind.
C flattering.
D genuine.
E envious.

/ 5

Answer these questions about the way words and phrases are used in the poem.

20. Which word is closest in meaning to "gauzy" (line 14)?

A Opaque
B Tiny
C Thin
D Reflective
E Shiny

21. Which word is closest in meaning to "behold" (line 16)?

A Understand
B View
C Grasp
D Approve
E Believe

22. The word "witty" (line 13) could be most accurately replaced by:

A friendly.
B amusing.
C beautiful.
D joyful.
E peculiar.

23. "'Tis" (line 2) and "ne'er" (line 6) are examples of:

A possessives.
B conjunctions.
C exclamations.
D adjectives.
E abbreviations.

24. What part of speech is "winding" (line 6)?

A Adverb
B Adjective
C Noun
D Pronoun
E Verb

/ 5

Carry on to the next question → →

Choose the right word or phrase to fill the gap. Circle the letter which matches the correct word.

25. Eleni **thinks** (A) **thought** (B) **has thought** (C) **thinked** (D) **thinking** (E) it would be easy to make a campfire.

26. Earlier, she had collected a pile of sticks **which** (A) **what** (B) **who** (C) **how** (D) **when** (E) she had arranged into a

27. wigwam shape. But they **must of** (A) **must have** (B) **must** (C) **should** (D) **would have** (E) been damp because

28. they refused to catch fire. Then, Eleni **saw** (A) **see** (B) **seen** (C) **sawed** (D) **seed** (E) a plume of smoke rising

29. from one corner. She added **all** (A) **more** (B) **fewer** (C) **most** (D) **none** (E) twigs to the pile. Suddenly

30. the flames seized hold **and** (A) **but** (B) **at** (C) **if** (D) **until** (E) the fire was alive!

/ 6

In this passage, there are some punctuation mistakes. Circle the letter which matches the part of the sentence with the mistake. If there's no mistake, circle N.

31. Whenever we go for a walk in the woods, Dad likes to lecture us on the surroundings. This

A B C D N

32. time it was on the way leaves turn brown in autumn: whereas last time we estimated the

A B C D N

33. height and age of the biggest trees. When he declared, We're going to Brook Valley today,"

A B C D N

34. Mita and I groaned: Brook Valley was by far the furthest, trail from the car park! We

A B C D N

35. deliberately dashed off in the opposite direction, racing each other to be first up the hill

A B C D N

/ 5

In this passage, there are some spelling mistakes. Circle the letter which matches the part of the sentence with the mistake. If there's no mistake, circle N.

36. Although the pantomime wasn't dew to start until 2 pm, we left in plenty of time.

A B C D N

37. (Trudy was worried about finding a decent place to park near the theatre.) It was a good idea,

A B C D N

38. because the snow was really thick and the traffick was crawling at a snail's pace. We

A B C D N

39. discovered a splendid space just behind a restaurant, close to the entrence. But, getting out

A B C D N

40. of the car, Dad slipped and hurt his ankle. He didn't complane much and enjoyed the show.

A B C D N

/ 5

Total / 40

End of Test

Assessment Test 3

Allow 40 minutes to do this test and work as quickly and as carefully as you can.

You can print **multiple-choice answer sheets** for these questions from our website — go to cgpbooks.co.uk/11plus/answer-sheets. If you'd prefer to answer them on the page, just follow the instructions in the question.

Read this passage carefully and answer the questions that follow.

Hadrian's Wall

Today, Rome is the capital city of Italy, but about 2,000 years ago it was the centre of the Roman Empire. The Roman Empire was the name given to the lands ruled by the Emperor; at its peak, it stretched from England to Egypt. One such Emperor was Hadrian, the man who was responsible for building Hadrian's Wall. Hadrian's Wall was built near England's border with Scotland, and marked the northernmost boundary of the Roman Empire. Construction started about 1900 years ago, and took about six years. Made from limestone, earth and clay, the wall was 3-6 metres high. At around 117 kilometres long, it's still the longest wall in Europe, although many parts have fallen into disrepair.

The reasons for building Hadrian's Wall are unclear. Some historians believe it was to stop invaders from North Britannia (Scotland), but others think it was used to control immigration and smuggling and to tax goods. Another theory is that it was built to show off Rome's might, as it could be seen for miles around.

Around 9,000 soldiers were needed to man the wall. These soldiers lived in large forts which had temples, granaries, bath houses and even hospitals. Apart from occasional attacks from the north, life on the wall was mostly peaceful.

After Hadrian's death, Emperor Antoninus Pius abandoned Hadrian's Wall and built the Antonine Wall, 160 kilometres further north. Antoninus believed that it would help the Romans conquer Scotland, but his efforts were fruitless and when he died, the soldiers retreated to Hadrian's Wall. The Romans left Britain around 1600 years ago, and by 1200 years ago, people had already started to reuse the stones from the wall in roads and other buildings, such as the monastery at Jarrow.

Answer these questions about the text that you've just read.
Circle the letter that matches the correct answer.

1. Which of the following best describes how the wall looks today?

A Fully intact
B Buried
C Demolished
D Partially broken down
E Larger than in Roman times

2. What did Hadrian's Wall mark?

A The English border
B The Scottish border
C The northern border of the Roman Empire
D Hadrian's kingdom
E The southern border of the Roman Empire

/ 2

3. According to the text, which of the following facilities weren't found in Roman forts near the wall?

A Places of worship
B Tax offices
C Medical facilities
D Storage for grain
E Washing facilities

4. During the Roman period, Hadrian's Wall was:

A attacked by the English.
B often fought over.
C always under fire.
D sometimes attacked.
E never attacked.

5. Why was the Antonine Wall constructed?

A To show how powerful Rome was
B To re-use stones from Hadrian's Wall
C To replace Hadrian's Wall
D To protect the Roman Empire from invaders from the north
E To extend the Roman Empire to the north

6. Which one of the following is not suggested as a possible reason for the building of Hadrian's Wall?

A To tax produce
B To demonstrate how powerful Rome was
C To stop attackers
D To increase immigration
E To limit smuggling

7. According to the passage, which of these statements about Hadrian's Wall is false?

A It's the longest wall in the world.
B Nobody really knows why Hadrian's Wall was built.
C It took less than 10 years to build.
D It took around 9,000 soldiers to occupy the wall.
E You can still see parts of the wall today.

/ 5

Carry on to the next question → →

Answer these questions about the way words and phrases are used in the passage.

8. In the context of the passage, which of these words is closest in meaning to "might" (line 10)?

A Maybe
B Ability
C Power
D Command
E Anger

9. Which of these words is closest in meaning to "retreated" (line 17)?

A Withdrew
B Sheltered
C Abandoned
D Escaped
E Defended

10. What is the meaning of the phrase "his efforts were fruitless" (line 17)?

A He made a lot of mistakes.
B He made a lot of enemies.
C He didn't get the credit he deserved.
D He wasted a lot of money.
E He was unsuccessful.

11. "at its peak, it stretched from England to Egypt." (lines 2-3).
Which of these words is a common noun?

A its
B peak
C stretched
D England
E Egypt

12. In the context of the passage, "marked" (line 4) and "tax" (line 10) are examples of which part of speech?

A Adjectives
B Verbs
C Nouns
D Adverbs
E Metaphors

/ 5

Read this passage carefully and answer the questions that follow.

Adapted from 'The Wind in the Willows'

The afternoon sun was getting low as the Rat sculled gently homewards in a dreamy mood, not paying much attention to Mole. But the Mole was very full of lunch, and self-satisfaction, and pride, and already quite at home in a boat (so he thought) and was getting a bit restless: and presently he said, 'Ratty! Please, *I* want to row, now!'

The Rat shook his head with a smile. 'Not yet, my young friend, wait till you've had a few lessons. It's not so easy as it looks.'

The Mole was quiet for a minute or two. But he began to feel more and more jealous of Rat, sculling so strongly and so easily along, and his pride began to whisper that he could do it every bit as well. He jumped up and seized the sculls, so suddenly, that the Rat, who was gazing out over the water, was taken by surprise and fell backwards off his seat with his legs in the air, while the triumphant Mole took his place and grabbed the sculls with entire confidence.

'Stop it!' cried the Rat. 'You can't do it! You'll have us over!'

The Mole flung his sculls back with a flourish, and made a great dig at the water. He missed the surface altogether, his legs flew up above his head, and he found himself lying on top of the prostrate Rat. Greatly alarmed, he made a grab at the side of the boat, and the next moment – sploosh!

Over went the boat, and he found himself struggling in the river.

by Kenneth Grahame

Answer these questions about the text that you've just read.
Circle the letter that matches the correct answer.

13. At what time of the day were Mole and Rat rowing?

A Early morning
B Late morning
C Early afternoon
D Late afternoon
E Late evening

14. Which statement about Mole is not true?

A He was in a dreamy mood.
B He was impatient.
C He had eaten lots.
D He wanted to row.
E He envied Rat.

/ 2

Carry on to the next question → →

15. Why does Rat not allow Mole to row?

A It was Rat's boat and he didn't want to share.
B They were nearly home.
C He thought Mole needed to practise first.
D He thought Mole would row too fast.
E He thought Mole was not a good rower.

16. Why was Mole jealous of Rat?

A Rat was not paying him any attention.
B Rat was a very skilful rower.
C Mole wanted to be a rat.
D Rat would not let him row.
E Rat had a boat.

17. What happened to Rat when Mole grabbed the sculls?

A He fell backwards into the boat.
B He fell on top of Mole.
C He fell into the water.
D He was knocked over by a scull.
E He fell onto the sculls.

18. Once Mole had the sculls, which one of the following things did not happen?

A Rat shouted at Mole.
B Mole missed the water with the sculls.
C Mole tried to show off with the sculls.
D Mole lost his balance and fell onto Rat.
E Mole accidentally hit Rat with the sculls.

19. Which adjective best describes Mole in lines 9-11?

A Reckless
B Jealous
C Bored
D Brave
E Impressive

/ 5

Answer these questions about the way words and phrases are used in the passage.

20. Mole felt "at home in a boat" (line 3). What does this expression mean?

A He felt warm.
B He felt lazy.
C He felt proud.
D He felt comfortable.
E He felt welcome.

21. Which of these is closest in meaning to "triumphant" (line 11)?

A Strong
B Victorious
C Foolish
D Boastful
E Lucky

22. Which of these is closest in meaning to "alarmed" (line 15)?

A Suspicious
B Concerned
C Noisy
D Upset
E Panicked

23. Mole's "pride began to whisper" (line 8). What type of phrase is this?

A A metaphor
B Alliteration
C A simile
D Personification
E A rhyme

24. What type of words are these?

young **restless** **jealous** **triumphant**

A Adverbs
B Pronouns
C Adjectives
D Nouns
E Verbs

/ 5

Carry on to the next question → →

In this passage, there are some spelling mistakes. Circle the letter which matches the part of the sentence with the mistake. If there's no mistake, circle N.

25. The local swimming club celebrated its tenth birthday today with a gala of unnusual events

A	B	C	D	N

26. which all club members were invited to attend. Fancy dress costumes were handed out, as

A	B	C	D	N

27. well as differentley coloured hats used to identify the four teams. All sorts of races took

A	B	C	D	N

28. place, includeing a raft race, a piggy-back relay and a watery treasure hunt at the bottom of

A	B	C	D	N

29. the pool. There was a brilliant buffet and the county team desined a cake shaped like a fish.

A	B	C	D	N

/ 5

Choose the right word or phrase to fill the gap. Circle the letter which matches the correct word.

30. Creating a rockery is a great project **for to that which from** budding gardeners.
A B C D E

31. **After Before Since Until During** you begin, find a good location for your rockery.
A B C D E

32. In that location, dig a shallow ditch. Put the soil **an onto in with between** a plastic
A B C D E

33. sheet, remove any weeds and throw away any stones **we I they you one** find. Place the large
A B C D E

34. rocks in natural positions, then put lots of soil **around under in through towards** them.
A B C D E

35. Finally, **digging dig dug digs have dug** holes between the rocks for your plants.
A B C D E

/ 6

In this passage, there are some punctuation mistakes. Circle the letter which matches the part of the sentence with the mistake. If there's no mistake, circle N.

36. "Are we nearly there yet," Maria wailed, peering into the darkness. "Not much longer,"

A	B	C	D	N

37. Mum replied; flicking on the wipers yet again. Seeing the Blackpool lights had seemed

A	B	C	D	N

38. a real treat, but the journey had taken forever. Maria had dozed off Dinesh had listened

A	B	C	D	N

39. to music on his headphones and, Grandad had chattered away endlessly. However, as they

A	B	C	D	N

40. turned a corner, a vivid blaze of flashing green, red and orange light greeted them at last.

A	B	C	D	N

/ 5

Total / 40

End of Test

Assessment Test 4

Allow 40 minutes to do this test and work as quickly and as carefully as you can.

You can print **multiple-choice answer sheets** for these questions from our website — go to cgpbooks.co.uk/11plus/answer-sheets. If you'd prefer to answer them on the page, just follow the instructions in the question.

Read this passage carefully and answer the questions that follow.

The Bizarre Bazaar

Michael stood in the freezing downpour, staring between the sodden canvas drapes of a market stall at a beautiful miniature elephant carved from ivory. He stepped under the deserted awning and picked up the ornament.

Immediately, his body tingled as if an electric current was flowing through him and he felt a wave of dizziness, forcing his eyes shut.

He opened his eyes to see a huge elephant charging towards him and leapt aside just in time. A much smaller elephant ran past, followed by two hunters carrying rifles. The large elephant charged onwards, unaware that its baby had become entangled in a clump of scrub. The baby elephant stood petrified as the hunters approached.

"There's no point shooting the baby," said the shorter of the hunters. "It doesn't have tusks. No tusks means no ivory to sell."

"True," said her taller companion. "Let's go after the adult elephant."

"No, Kevin! Any second now, she'll notice her baby isn't with her. All we have to do is wait." She smirked and held up her gun.

Michael watched, horrified, as the adult elephant stopped and turned. The hunters raised their rifles. He ran towards them, waving his arms and yelling loudly. The terrified baby elephant thrashed wildly and freed itself from the scrub and both elephants charged off into the distance. The hunters stared in amazement.

The air shimmered and, seconds later, Michael was back in the bazaar. His heart was pounding and he was disorientated. He looked down and cried out when he saw his empty hands; the ivory ornament had disappeared. Michael was bewildered for a moment and then it hit him: by saving the elephant he had prevented the ornament ever being made.

Answer these questions about the text that you've just read.
Circle the letter that matches the correct answer.

1. Which of the following statements is not true?

A Michael saw the ornament on a market stall.
B Michael was the only customer at the stall.
C It was a hot summer's day.
D The elephant ornament was not very big.
E The ornament was carved from elephant tusks.

/ 1

2. Why did the elephant charge towards Michael?

A It wanted to hurt him.
B It thought he was going to hurt the young elephant.
C It was running after its baby.
D It was frightened by his yelling.
E It was fleeing from the hunters.

3. Why did the hunters decide to spare the young elephant?

A They were kind-hearted.
B It was illegal to shoot young elephants.
C They didn't want to anger the adult elephant.
D They would not make any money by killing it.
E Michael scared it away.

4. Why was Michael "horrified" (line 15)?

A He was afraid the hunter would shoot him.
B He was afraid the elephant would hurt the hunters.
C He was afraid the elephant would hurt him.
D He was afraid the hunters would shoot the adult elephant.
E He was afraid the hunters would shoot the baby elephant.

5. How do you think Michael felt in line 20?

A Exhausted
B Happy
C Confused
D Excited
E Sick

6. What does Michael realise at the end of the story?

A He has mislaid the ornament.
B He has changed history.
C He saved the hunters from the angry elephant.
D He imagined the ornament.
E His adventure was just a dream.

7. Which of the following facts is not given in the story?

A The name of the shorter hunter.
B The name of the main character.
C The substance the ornament was made from.
D The reason the hunters were hunting the elephant.
E The number of hunters.

/ 6

Carry on to the next question → →

Answer these questions about the way words and phrases are used in the passage.

8. Which of these words is closest in meaning to "thrashed" (line 16)?

A Flailed
B Jumped
C Snorted
D Spun
E Stamped

9. The word "petrified" (line 9) could most accurately be replaced by:

A terrified.
B alarmed.
C worried.
D panicked.
E dismayed.

10. The word "smirked" (line 14) could most accurately be replaced by:

A smiled.
B laughed.
C snarled.
D stopped.
E frowned.

11. In the sentence, "the ivory ornament had disappeared" (lines 20-21), which word is a noun?

A the
B ivory
C ornament
D had
E disappeared

12. "his body tingled as if an electric current was flowing through him" (line 4). What technique is used here?

A A metaphor
B A simile
C Personification
D A homophone
E Alliteration

/ 5

Read this passage carefully and answer the questions that follow.

An extract from 'The Wizard of Oz'

It was very dark, and the wind howled horribly around her, but Dorothy found she was riding quite easily. After the first few whirls around, and one other time when the house tipped badly, she felt as if she were being rocked gently, like a baby in a cradle.

Toto did not like it. He ran about the room, now here, now there, barking loudly; but Dorothy sat quite still on the floor and waited to see what would happen. Once Toto got too near the open trap door, and fell in; and at first the little girl thought she had lost him. But soon she saw one of his ears sticking up through the hole, for the strong pressure of the air was keeping him up so that he could not fall. She crept to the hole, caught Toto by the ear, and dragged him into the room again, afterward closing the trap door so that no more accidents could happen.

Hour after hour passed away, and slowly Dorothy got over her fright; but she felt quite lonely, and the wind shrieked so loudly all about her that she nearly became deaf. At first she had wondered if she would be dashed to pieces when the house fell again; but as the hours passed and nothing terrible happened, she stopped worrying and resolved to wait calmly and see what the future would bring.

At last she crawled over the swaying floor to her bed, and lay down upon it; and Toto followed and lay down beside her. In spite of the swaying of the house and the wailing of the wind, Dorothy soon closed her eyes and fell fast asleep.

by L. Frank Baum

Answer these questions about the text that you've just read.
Circle the letter that matches the correct answer.

13. What natural event is Dorothy caught up in?

A An earthquake
B An avalanche
C A lightning storm
D A tornado
E A blizzard

14. Which of the following statements does not describe the movement of the house?

A It rocks.
B It sways.
C At the beginning the house revolves.
D It tips upside down.
E It moves quite smoothly.

/ 2

Carry on to the next question → →

15. What caused Toto to fall through the trap door?

A It was dark.
B The house tipped badly.
C He ran too close to the trap door.
D He was playing a game with Dorothy.
E He was dragged in by the air pressure.

16. What prevented Toto from being lost when he fell through the trap door?

A He landed on the floor of the cellar.
B Dorothy caught him by the ear.
C His ear got caught on the trap door.
D He was blown back up through the trap door.
E The air beneath the house was pushing him upwards.

17. Which of the following statements is true?
Once she had rescued Toto, Dorothy was worried:

A that she would be killed when the house fell back to the ground.
B about what the future might bring.
C that the house would tip and she would be injured.
D that she wouldn't be able to sleep.
E that she would be killed if she fell from the house.

18. Which of these words best describes how Dorothy feels at the end of the passage?

A Composed
B Frightened
C Agitated
D Lonely
E Energetic

19. When Dorothy falls asleep, which of these statements is true?

A The house had stopped rocking.
B It was night time.
C She was worried about the future.
D The house was still rocking.
E The wind had died down.

/ 5

Answer these questions about the way words and phrases are used in the passage.

20. Which word could best replace "resolved" in the phrase "resolved to wait calmly" (line 13)?

A Refused
B Persuaded
C Decided
D Forced
E Attempted

21. Which word is closest in meaning to "pressure" (line 7)?

A Gravity
B Force
C Firmness
D Constraint
E Atmosphere

22. "Dorothy found she was riding quite easily" (lines 1-2).
What does this sentence mean?

A It was as if Dorothy was on a horse.
B Dorothy didn't feel queasy from the tipping of the house.
C Dorothy was able to stand up despite the movement of the house.
D Dorothy was sliding gently from one side of the room to the other.
E Dorothy realised she was coping with the movement.

23. "the wind shrieked so loudly" (line 11).
What technique is being used here?

A A simile
B A metaphor
C Onomatopoeia
D Personification
E Alliteration

24. What type of word is "terrible" (line 13)?

A Adjective
B Verb
C Adverb
D Noun
E Preposition

/ 5

Carry on to the next question → →

In this passage, there are some spelling mistakes. Circle the letter which matches the part of the sentence with the mistake. If there's no mistake, circle N.

25. The fire alarm peirced the quiet of the fire station. Chanda's body tingled with excitement;

A **B** **C** **D** **N**

26. this was the moment she had been training for! Racing to the scarlet fire engine, Chanda felt

A **B** **C** **D** **N**

27. aprehensive, yet confident. The journey was swift and the engine swerved into a car park.

A **B** **C** **D** **N**

28. Chanda dashed into the blazing building and heared faint calls for help. Gingerly she inched

A **B** **C** **D** **N**

29. along the smoke-filled corridor until, finally, she was able to rescue the terriffied child.

A **B** **C** **D** **N**

/ 5

In this passage, there are some punctuation mistakes. Circle the letter which matches the part of the sentence with the mistake. If there's no mistake, circle N.

30. Good afternoon pupils and staff I am hoping to earn your vote today to become the

A **B** **C** **D** **N**

31. newest member of the school council. Im a responsible, dedicated and enthusiastic pupil.

A **B** **C** **D** **N**

32. Since I came to this school four, years ago, I have volunteered as a librarian, participated in

A **B** **C** **D** **N**

33. drama productions, organised charity events and even mentored younger pupils? Finally, I

A **B** **C** **D** **N**

34. have a perfect attendance record. What more could you look for in a pupil representative.

A **B** **C** **D** **N**

/ 5

Choose the right word or phrase to fill the gap. Circle the letter which matches the correct word.

35. There were mixed feelings this week as residents **here** (A) **hear** (B) **heard** (C) **hearing** (D) **herd** (E) that a

36. holiday park would be built in local woodland. No one knew **whom** (A) **whose** (B) **who's** (C) **who** (D) **which** (E)

37. had given permission to **sell** (A) **sale** (B) **sail** (C) **sold** (D) **selling** (E) the land in the ancient hundred-acre forest,

38. **furthermore** (A) **but** (B) **despite** (C) **when** (D) **finally** (E) the developers had already started the disruptive

39. building work. **All** (A) **None** (B) **Everyone** (C) **Some** (D) **The majority** (E) of residents are against the project,

40. although some can **saw** (A) **view** (B) **seeing** (C) **see** (D) **seen** (E) the benefits of increased tourism in the area.

/ 6

Total / 40

End of Test

Assessment Test 5

Allow 40 minutes to do this test and work as quickly and as carefully as you can.

You can print **multiple-choice answer sheets** for these questions from our website — go to cgpbooks.co.uk/11plus/answer-sheets. If you'd prefer to answer them on the page, just follow the instructions in the question.

Read this passage carefully and answer the questions that follow.

Echo and Narcissus

Narcissus was a Greek hunter who was renowned for his beauty. Countless women came to his home town of Thespiae to seduce him, which made Narcissus very arrogant. He rejected all of his admirers, because he thought that none of them were good enough.

Narcissus often hunted for deer in the forests. These forests were full of nymphs, divine creatures who kept the plants, trees and animals alive. One nymph, named Echo, fell in love with Narcissus, but he rejected her as well.

With her heart broken, Echo fled to a secret spring, where she faded away. Nemesis, a powerful goddess, saw how Narcissus had treated Echo, and decided to take revenge.

One day, Nemesis lured Narcissus to the spring where Echo had died. As he approached the water, Narcissus glimpsed an attractive face in the water and, thinking it was a beautiful water spirit, he fell in love with it. He bent down to kiss the spirit, but the water rippled and it vanished.

When the water became still, the spirit returned. Again, Narcissus tried to touch it, and again it disappeared. When the spirit returned for a third time, Narcissus just gazed intently at the face.

The sun rose and set many times, but still Narcissus stayed by the spring, growing weaker and weaker, wasting away because he didn't want to leave. Without food or sleep, he rapidly weakened and died. On the bank of the spring where his body had been, a white flower sprouted and blossomed, and this flower bears the name narcissus.

Answer these questions about the text that you've just read.
Circle the letter that matches the correct answer.

1. Why did Narcissus reject his admirers?

   A He thought he was better than them.
   B He didn't think that he was good enough for them.
   C He didn't think they were attractive enough.
   D He didn't think they were wealthy enough.
   E He thought he didn't need a wife.

2. According to the passage, what are nymphs?

   A Gods that planted trees.
   B Heavenly beings that tended to the forests.
   C Gardeners that looked after divine creatures.
   D Hunters that protected the forests from deer.
   E Spirits that created magical forests.

/ 2

3. Which of these statements is true?

   A Nemesis was a nymph.
   B Narcissus fell in love with Echo.
   C Narcissus did not fall in love with Echo.
   D Echo took revenge on Narcissus.
   E Nemesis was rejected by Narcissus.

4. Why do you think Echo ran away to the spring?

   A To look after the trees, plants and animals.
   B She wanted to see Narcissus.
   C She was upset and wanted to be alone.
   D Nemesis told her to go there.
   E She was meeting Nemesis there.

5. Why did the face Narcissus saw in the water keep disappearing?

   A It was afraid of Narcissus.
   B It did not love Narcissus.
   C It was a trap set by Nemesis.
   D It was Echo's ghost.
   E It was a reflection.

6. How long did Narcissus stay by the spring?

   A Weeks
   B Days
   C Hours
   D Years
   E Forever

7. What do you think this myth is a warning against?

   A Talking to strangers
   B Being too attractive
   C Falling in love
   D Telling lies
   E Being obsessed with how you look

/ 5

Carry on to the next question → →

Answer these questions about the way words and phrases are used in the passage.

8. Which of these words is closest in meaning to "renowned" (line 1)?

A Welcomed
B Worshipped
C Admired
D Cursed
E Famous

9. Which of these words is closest in meaning to "arrogant" (line 2)?

A Powerful
B Angry
C Confident
D Conceited
E Courageous

10. Which of these words is closest in meaning to "lured" (line 9)?

A Dragged
B Tricked
C Enticed
D Directed
E Walked

11. Which one of these sentences contains a proper noun?

A Without food or sleep, he eventually died.
B When the water became still, the spirit returned.
C He just gazed intently at the reflection.
D Countless women came to Thespiae.
E He bent down to kiss the spirit.

12. "kept" (line 5) and "gazed" (line 13) are examples of which part of speech?

A Adjectives
B Nouns
C Verbs
D Adverbs
E Metaphors

/ 5

Read this passage carefully and answer the questions that follow.

An extract from 'The Jungle Book'

"Man!" he snapped. "A man's cub. Look!"

Directly in front of him, holding on by a low branch, stood a naked brown baby who could just walk, as soft and as dimpled a little atom as ever came to a wolf's cave at night. He looked up into Father Wolf's face and laughed.

"Is that a man's cub?" said Mother Wolf. "I have never seen one. Bring it here."

A wolf accustomed to moving his own cubs can, if necessary, mouth an egg without breaking it, and though Father Wolf's jaws closed right on the child's back not a tooth even scratched the skin, as he laid it down among the cubs.

"How little! How naked, and — how bold!" said Mother Wolf, softly. The baby was pushing his way between the cubs to get close to the warm hide. "Ahai! He is taking his meal with the others. And so this is a man's cub. Now, was there ever a wolf that could boast of a man's cub among her children?"

"I have heard now and again of such a thing, but never in our pack or in my time," said Father Wolf. "He is altogether without hair, and I could kill him with a touch of my foot. But see, he looks up and is not afraid."

The moonlight was blocked out of the mouth of the cave, for Shere Khan's great square head and shoulders were thrust into the entrance. Tabaqui, behind him, was squeaking: "My Lord, my Lord, it went in here!"

by Rudyard Kipling

Answer these questions about the text that you've just read.
Circle the letter that matches the correct answer.

13. Why do the wolves call the child a "man's cub" (line 1)?

A They know whose baby it is.
B A baby wolf is called a "cub".
C They are scared of the child.
D It does not have any hair.
E They plan to take it back to its parents.

14. How does the reader know that the child is not a new-born baby?

A The child can walk.
B The child can talk.
C The child has hair.
D The child isn't afraid.
E The child is too big for Father Wolf to carry.

/ 2

Carry on to the next question → →

15. How does Father Wolf pick the baby up?

A Roughly
B Angrily
C Gently
D Fiercely
E Carelessly

16. Why does Father Wolf say "I could kill him with a touch of my foot" (line 13)?

A He is threatening the child because he does not like humans.
B He is explaining how small and weak the baby is.
C He is angry that the child is not afraid of him.
D He wants to frighten the child to make him less bold.
E He wants to punish the child for eating the cubs' food.

17. Which two of the following is given as a reason for the baby pushing his way in amongst the cubs?

1 He is afraid of Father Wolf.
2 He is hiding from Shere Khan.
3 He is looking for food.
4 He is trying to get warm.
5 He wants to go to sleep.

A 1 and 5
B 3 and 4
C 2 and 3
D 2 and 4
E 3 and 5

18. Which of the following statements is not true?

A Mother Wolf is intrigued by the child.
B Mother Wolf is proud that the child is amongst her cubs.
C Mother and Father Wolf have cubs of their own.
D Father Wolf discovered the child.
E Mother and Father Wolf have seen human children before.

19. Who do you think Tabaqui is?

A Shere Khan's lord
B Shere Khan's sidekick
C The owner of the cave
D The child's father
E A friend of Father Wolf

/ 5

Answer these questions about the way words and phrases are used in the passage.

20. Which of these phrases is closest in meaning to "accustomed to" (line 6)?

A Aware of
B Unfamiliar with
C Attempting to
D Cautious of
E Used to

21. The word "hide" (line 10) could most accurately be replaced by:

A Skin
B Conceal
C Shelter
D Secret
E Animal

22. Which word is closest in meaning to "thrust" (line 16)?

A Placed
B Nudged
C Shoved
D Located
E Pointed

23. "But see, he looks up and is not afraid." (lines 13-14)
Which of these words is a preposition?

A But
B see
C looks
D up
E afraid

24. What part of speech is the word "square" in the phrase
"Shere Khan's great square head" (line 15)?

A Noun
B Adverb
C Verb
D Adjective
E Preposition

/ 5

Carry on to the next question →→

In this passage, there are some spelling mistakes. Circle the letter which matches the part of the sentence with the mistake. If there's no mistake, circle N.

25. I went to the Natural History Museum in London yesterday and it was fascinating! We caught

A B C D N

26. the train and the tube to get there. The architectare was spectacular, but most impressive

A B C D N

27. of all were the dinosoar exhibits. I can't believe how enormous some of the creatures were!

A B C D N

28. I was most interested in the T-Rex with its gigantic head and hind legs, yet rediculously tiny

A B C D N

29. arms. We went to the gift shop afterwards and I bought a T-Rex pencil for my best freind.

A B C D N

/ 5

Choose the right word or phrase to fill the gap. Circle the letter which matches the correct word.

30. Lara had been **gave got given had taken** a metal detector for her birthday. The first time she

A B C D E

31. used it **should of should have must has was must have** been a very exciting day. She packed

A B C D E

32. a picnic and the detector and ran **from before at for behind** the bus which would take her to

A B C D E

33. the beach. She eagerly hopped off at her stop, but when she **open opened undo opens opening**

A B C D E

34. her bag, Lara realised that she had **forgot forget brung bringed forgotten** the battery pack

A B C D E

35. for the metal detector. All she could do was **ate eaten eat eating eated** her picnic.

A B C D E

/ 6

In this passage, there are some punctuation mistakes. Circle the letter which matches the part of the sentence with the mistake. If there's no mistake, circle N.

36. "It's arrived!" Aishas' stomach flipped in excitement and she noticed that her hands were

A B C D N

37. shaking. This was the letter she had been waiting for. "What is it." her younger sister asked.

A B C D N

38. Aisha turned the envelope nervously in her fingers. "Open it!" her sister demanded excitedly

A B C D N

39. She took a deep breath to calm her nerves. She hoped that the envelope contained good news.

A B C D N

40. Fingers trembling Aisha, tore it open. Inside was a letter saying she'd made the county team!

A B C D N

/ 5

Total / 40

End of Test

Assessment Test 6

Allow 40 minutes to do this test and work as quickly and as carefully as you can.

You can print **multiple-choice answer sheets** for these questions from our website — go to cgpbooks.co.uk/11plus/answer-sheets. If you'd prefer to answer them on the page, just follow the instructions in the question.

Read this passage carefully and answer the questions that follow.

The Blizzard

It came without warning. The day had started cold but bright, the sunlight sharpening the edges of the trees against the sky. Towards noon, leaden clouds gathered suddenly and with them the first flurries of snow. The wind sprang from nowhere, whipping the flakes to a frenzy, and within minutes the countryside was obscured.

High above the village, Achak pulled his sister closer in the darkness. When the blizzard began, they had searched frantically for shelter, Alawa clinging to Achak's hand as he dragged her deeper into the forest where the trees would provide some kind of break against the icy winds and drifting snow. Almost blinded and half frozen, he had seen it: a dark slash against the white. Exhausted, the two children had crawled into the temporary protection of the cave. Alawa's tiny body shook violently despite her furs. Gradually the combined warmth of their bodies stilled the tremors and she fell asleep, still clutching the bag of herbs they had been collecting in the forest when the storm started.

Achak laid her gently on the ground and went to the cave entrance. Outside, the wind had stilled. The sky was now a deep magenta as the sun sank swiftly behind the mountains. Beneath him, the snow was a white blanket making the once-familiar countryside unrecognisable. Great drifts altered the landscape, destroying all sense of direction. From the depths of the forest a single howl ripped through the icy air, and was answered once, twice, three times. Uneasily, Achak made his decision. They would have to remain until morning.

Answer these questions about the text that you've just read.
Circle the letter that matches the correct answer.

1. When did the blizzard start?

   A First thing in the morning
   B Around midnight
   C Around midday
   D As it got dark
   E Mid-morning

2. Why did Achak drag Alawa deeper into the forest?

   A To get back to the safety of the village.
   B To find more herbs.
   C To get away from the wolves.
   D To find shelter from the blizzard.
   E He couldn't see where he was going in the darkness.

/ 2

3. How did Achak try to warm up Alawa?

A He put his fur coat around her.
B He sat very close to her.
C He gave her some herbs.
D He held her hand.
E He lit a fire.

4. What were the children doing in the forest before the blizzard?

A Looking for shelter.
B Hunting for wolves.
C Collecting firewood.
D Collecting plants.
E Playing in the snow.

5. Which of these statements is true of Achak's view from the cave?

A He couldn't make out any familiar landmarks because of the snow.
B He could see a wolf prowling nearby.
C It was dark and he couldn't see the village.
D He could see his village below him now the blizzard had stopped.
E The sun was rising beyond the mountains.

6. Which of these descriptions of the weather is true?

A The day started warm but got colder.
B It snowed all day.
C The blizzard started gradually.
D It was clear and then started raining.
E The winds were strong during the blizzard.

7. Choose the answer which puts the events from the story in the order in which they happen.

1 Alawa and Achak sheltered in the cave.
2 Darkness approached.
3 The children went deeper into the forest.
4 There was brilliant sunshine.
5 The blizzard started.

A 4, 5, 1, 2, 3
B 3, 5, 1, 4, 2
C 4, 5, 3, 1, 2
D 4, 5, 2, 3, 1
E 4, 5, 1, 3, 2

/ 5

Carry on to the next question →→

Answer these questions about the way words and phrases are used in the passage.

8. Which of these phrases could best replace "obscured" (line 4)?

A Frozen
B Forgotten
C Destroyed
D Hidden
E Flattened

9. What colour is "magenta" (line 14)?

A Blue-grey
B Greyish-green
C Orangey-yellow
D Purplish-pink
E Blackish-blue

10. Why do you think the writer describes the cave as "a dark slash against the white" (line 8)?

A The cave was cold.
B Snow had hidden the entrance to the cave.
C The dark mouth of the cave stood out against the snow.
D The cave's entrance was in a clearing where there was no snow.
E The cave looked threatening.

11. "Gradually the combined warmth of their bodies stilled the tremors" (line 10).
Which word is an adverb?

A Gradually
B combined
C their
D stilled
E tremors

12. "the snow was a white blanket" (line 15).
What technique is this an example of?

A Personification
B Onomatopoeia
C Metaphor
D Alliteration
E Simile

/ 5

Read this poem carefully and answer the questions that follow.

Adapted from 'Travel'

I should like to rise and go
Where the golden apples grow;—

Where below another sky
Parrot islands anchored lie,
And, watched by cockatoos and goats,
Lonely Crusoes building boats;—

Where in sunshine reaching out
Eastern cities, miles about,
Are with mosque and minaret
Among sandy gardens set,
And the rich goods from near and far
Hang for sale in the bazaar;—

Where the Great Wall round China goes,
And on one side the desert blows,
And with the bell and voice and drum,
Cities on the other hum;—

Where are forests, hot as fire,
Wide as England, tall as a spire,
Where the knotty crocodile
Lies and blinks in the Nile,
And the red flamingo flies
Hunting fish before his eyes;—

Where in jungles, near and far,
Man-devouring tigers are,
Lying close and giving ear
Lest the hunt be drawing near.

by Robert Louis Stevenson

Answer these questions about the text that you've just read.
Circle the letter that matches the correct answer.

13. What is the poem about?

A The poet is describing all the places he has visited.
B The poet is imagining the places he would like to visit.
C The poet is describing places he would not like to visit.
D The poet is talking about where he lives.
E The poet is persuading people to travel to these places.

14. What does the poet mean when he says "below another sky" (line 3)?

A On a different planet
B During better weather
C In another country
D In a different climate
E On the ground

/ 2

Carry on to the next question → →

15. Which of these statements about the eastern cities is not true?

A The markets sell only local produce.
B There are religious buildings.
C They are very large.
D They are sunny.
E They have sandy gardens.

16. Which of these best describes what the crocodile is doing?

A Lying with his eyes closed
B Hiding in the water
C Moving his eyes from side to side
D Watching the fish
E Watching the flamingo fly

17. What mood does the poet create in lines 15-16?

A Serene
B Bustling
C Exotic
D Dangerous
E Carefree

18. Which of these best describes what the tiger is doing?

A Hiding from people
B Hunting for prey
C Lying still and blinking
D Waiting to catch people
E Lying and listening for hunters

19. Which of these places is not mentioned in the poem?

A Tropical islands
B Deserted cities
C Expansive forests
D Exotic orchards
E Colourful markets

/ 5

Answer these questions about the way words and phrases are used in the poem.

20. What is a "spire" (line 18)?

A A tower with a pointed roof
B A mountain with steep cliffs
C A stone statue
D A tower with a turret
E An elaborate chimney

21. "Hunting fish before his eyes" (line 22).
Which of these words is a verb?

A Hunting
B fish
C before
D his
E eyes

22. What is meant by the word "devouring" (line 24)?

A Threatening
B Tasting
C Roaring
D Eating
E Hunting

23. What kind of word is "China" (line 13)?

A Common noun
B Abstract noun
C Proper noun
D Adverb
E Conjunction

24. "forests, hot as fire" (line 17).
What technique is this an example of?

A Metaphor
B Personification
C Onomatopoeia
D Alliteration
E Simile

/ 5

Carry on to the next question → →

In this passage, there are some punctuation mistakes. Circle the letter which matches the part of the sentence with the mistake. If there's no mistake, circle N.

25. Are you a budding author? If so, make sure to enter this years creative writing competition.

A	B	C	D	N

26. You still have four weeks before the closing date. Poetry, horror, romance, and myth are

A	B	C	D	N

27. just a few of the genres you could choose from! Your competition entry will be judged

A	B	C	D	N

28. by a famous author, and the winner (along with all the short-listed entries will be published

A	B	C	D	N

29. in the 'bumper Book of Young Writers'. So what are you waiting for? Pick up that pen!

A	B	C	D	N

/ 5

Choose the right word or phrase to fill the gap. Circle the letter which matches the correct word.

30. People's lives could be in danger **where** **so** **while** **when** **if** £3 million is not found

A B C D E

31. to fund the air ambulance. **They're** **Their** **There** **Their's** **There's** is a huge demand

A B C D E

32. for the two helicopters, **which** **who** **when** **whom** **what** were called out twenty-three times

A B C D E

33. **on** **over** **until** **into** **by** the holiday period. The money is needed for fuel, training and

A B C D E

34. salaries, so it is a vital cause. A spokesperson **said** **says** **say** **saying** **will say** today,

A B C D E

35. "We must involve **more** **few** **lots** **most** **most of** people in fundraising activities."

A B C D E

/ 6

In this passage, there are some spelling mistakes. Circle the letter which matches the part of the sentence with the mistake. If there's no mistake, circle N.

36 Not sure how you are going to fill your summer holidays? Look no further than 'Activity

A	B	C	D	N

37. Holidays'. We can offer you the choise of an action-packed experience for a day, week or even

A	B	C	D	N

38. the whole holiday. Make new friends, learn new skills and build up your confidance and

A	B	C	D	N

39. independence. Test your nerve with a fantastic range of thrilling indoor and outdoor challinges:

A	B	C	D	N

40. cooking, diveing, archery, pottery and much more — there really is something for everyone!

A	B	C	D	N

/ 5

Total / 40

End of Test

Glossary

abbreviation	A shortened version of a word, e.g. "bike" instead of "bicycle".
adjective	A word that describes a noun, e.g. "beautiful morning", "frosty lawn".
adverb	A word that describes a verb or an adjective, e.g. "She laughed happily."
alliteration	The repetition of a sound at the beginning of words within a phrase, e.g. "Loopy Lois likes lipstick."
antonym	A word that has the opposite meaning to another, e.g. "good" and "bad".
comparative	A word that compares one thing with another, e.g. "shorter", "worse".
conjunction	A word that joins two clauses, e.g. "and", "but".
fiction	Text that has been made up by the author, about imaginary people and events.
homographs	Words that are spelt the same, but have different meanings, e.g. row (argue/paddle).
homophones	Words that sound the same, but mean different things, e.g. "hair" and "hare".
idiom	A phrase which doesn't literally mean what it says, e.g. "raining cats and dogs".
imagery	Language that creates a vivid picture in the reader's mind.
irony	When a writer says the opposite of what they mean, or when the opposite happens to what the reader expects.
metaphor	A way of describing something by saying that it is something else, e.g. "John's legs were lead weights."
non-fiction	Text that is about facts and real people and events.
noun	A word that names something, e.g. "Paul", "scissors", "flock", "loyalty".
onomatopoeia	When words sound like the noise they describe, e.g. "pop", "bang", "squelch".
personification	A way of describing something by giving it human feelings and characteristics, e.g. "The cruel wind plucked remorselessly at my threadbare clothes."
prefix	Letters that can be put in front of a word to change its meaning, e.g. "unlock".
preposition	A word that tells you how things are related, e.g. "in", "above", "before".
pronoun	Words that can be used instead of nouns, e.g. "I", "you", "he", "it".
proverb	A short well-known phrase that may give advice, e.g. "There's no point crying over spilt milk."
rhetorical question	A question that doesn't need an answer, e.g. "When will they learn?"
simile	A way of describing something by comparing it to something else, e.g. "The stars were like a thousand diamonds, glittering in the sky."
subject	The person or thing doing the action of a verb, e.g. "Jo laughed", "the bird flew".
suffix	Letters that can be put after a word to change its meaning, e.g. "playful".
superlative	A word that refers to the most or least of a group of things, e.g. "the best team".
synonym	A word with a similar meaning to another word, e.g. "big" and "huge".
verb	An action or being word, e.g. "I run", "he went", "we think".